Crazy Creatures

OF THE WORLD

BY JOANNE MATTERN

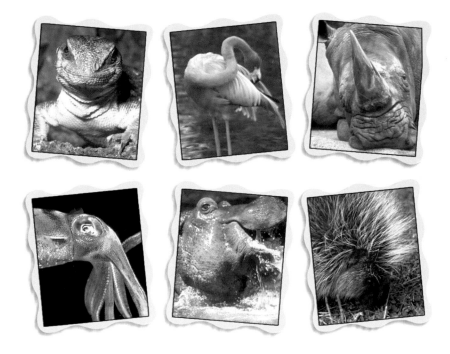

Perfection Learning®

BOOK DESIGN: Jan M. Michalson

ABOUT THE AUTHOR

Joanne Mattern is the author of many books for children. Her favorite topics include animals, biography, and history. She especially likes writing nonfiction because it allows her to bring real people, places, and events to life. "I firmly believe that everything in the world is a story waiting to be told."

Along with writing, Joanne enjoys speaking to school and community groups about the topics in her books. She is also a huge baseball fan and enjoys music and needlework.

Joanne lives in the Hudson Valley of New York State with her husband and young daughter. The family also includes a greyhound and two cats, and "more animals are always welcome!"

IMAGE CREDITS

All images are Corel Professional Photos except Image Technologies: cover right, p. 2; ArtToday (www.arttoday.com): pp. 1 green, yellow, and gray borders, 8, 56 middle green border; Digital Stock: pp. 1 bottom right, 10 top, 21, 22, 23, 35, 56 bottom left; Corbis: pp. 47, 50.

© Joe McDonald/CORBIS: p. 9; © Lynwood M. Chace, The National Audubon Society Collection/PR: p. 11; © Tom McHugh, The National Audubon Society Collection/PR: p. 30; © Ralph A. Clevenger/CORBIS: p. 44; © David T. Roberts, The National Audubon Society Collection/PR: p. 52.

Contents

Chapter One

Mammals

Mammals are special kinds of animals. They are *warm-blooded*. That means they can control their body temperatures.

Mammals also give birth to live young instead of laying eggs. And they nurse their young with milk from the mothers' bodies.

Mammals have something else in common. Their bodies usually have hair or fur.

Cats, dogs, bears, elephants, and monkeys are all mammals. Guess what? You're a mammal too!

Let's meet some really crazy mammals. All these animals are really strange in one way or another!

Anteaters have crazy-looking bodies. But their bodies are just right for finding ants to eat.

Anteaters have short legs. Their bodies are close to the ground. This helps anteaters smell and hear insects.

These mammals also have long, sharp claws. They use them to rip open ant nests and termite mounds.

Anteaters' tongues are probably the craziest of all. They are long and thin. So they're just right for catching ants!

Anteaters shove their tongues deep into ants' nests. Sharp hooks on their tongues pick up ants. Then the anteaters slurp all those tasty ants back into their mouths.

Armadillos

A famous naturalist named John Audubon once said that armadillos looked like pigs in turtles' shells. These crazy creatures are covered by hard shells. Their shells are called *carapaces.*

Armadillos lose body heat through their shells. Their shells have no fur or hair to keep heat inside.

So armadillos must live in warm places. They make their homes in South and Central America and the southern United States.

These mammals never have to wonder how many babies they will have. Armadillos always give birth to four *identical* babies. That means they are exactly alike. And the babies are either all males or all females.

Armadillos do a crazy thing when they're frightened. They jump straight up in the air. They can jump 1 to 2 feet high. When they land, armadillos run away.

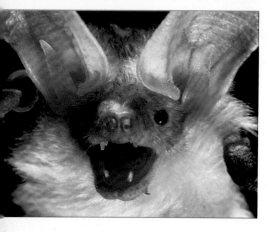

Birds and insects aren't the only animals that fly. Bats can too! In fact, they are the only mammals that can fly.

Bats have funny-looking faces. Their ears may be very big. Or their noses often have flaps of skin on them. But these crazy ears and noses help bats find insects to eat.

Bats use a system called *echolocation.* They make high-pitched squeaking noises. These sounds are pushed out through their noses.

Then bats' ears pick up the echoes that bounce back. These echoes tell bats where insects are flying. They also tell bats where objects are. Then bats can avoid running into them.

Bats fly at night. During the day, they sleep. Bats hang upside down by their toes. They wrap their wings around their bodies when they go to sleep.

Star-Nosed Moles

Most moles spend their lives underground. But star-nosed moles live in streams and ponds.

The crazy-looking star shapes on the moles' noses are made of 22 feelers. These feelers are very sensitive.

Moles poke their feelers around to find food. The feelers also cover their noses while the moles are swimming underwater.

Their feelers work so well that the star-nosed moles don't need to see where they're going. In fact, these crazy creatures are almost blind!

Porcupines

Porcupines have a crazy way of defending themselves. Their bodies are covered with long, sharp quills. If an attacker touches a porcupine or is hit by a porcupine's tail, the quills will stick in the attacker's skin. This is very painful!

Porcupines are quiet animals. They spend most of their days eating tree bark.

Skunks act pretty crazy when they get mad. When they face danger, they stamp their feet. Then they hiss and growl.

If attackers still haven't gone away, skunks spray them with a bad-smelling liquid called *musk*. Few animals will stay around after they're covered with horrible-smelling skunk musk!

Skunks are *nocturnal*. They sleep most of the day and come out at night to eat. Their favorite foods are insects and worms they dig out of the ground. Skunks also eat nuts, fruit, birds' eggs, and other small animals.

Opossums

Opossums are *marsupials*. These are a special kind of mammal. Opossums are the only *species*, or type, of marsupials in North America.

Opossum babies are not fully developed when they are born. And they are too small to live on their own. So the babies crawl into a pouch on their mother's stomach.

After several weeks, the babies are big enough to come out of the pouch. But they still need to stay close to their mothers. So they hitch a ride on their moms' backs! The mothers walk around and climb trees with a row of tiny babies hanging onto their fur.

Hippopotamuses

Hippos are more at home in the water than on land. If hippos do not stay wet, their skin dries out. Then they will die.

Staying in the water also helps hippos stay cool in the hot African sun. And the water supports the hippos' heavy bodies. Hippos can weigh 2,500 pounds.

Hippos' bodies are well-suited to stay in water. Their eyes and nostrils stick up so the animals can see and breathe while they are in deep water.

Hippos can also hold their breath for up to 6 minutes. Baby hippos are even born underwater! Hippopotamuses are related to pigs. Sometimes they are called *water pigs.*

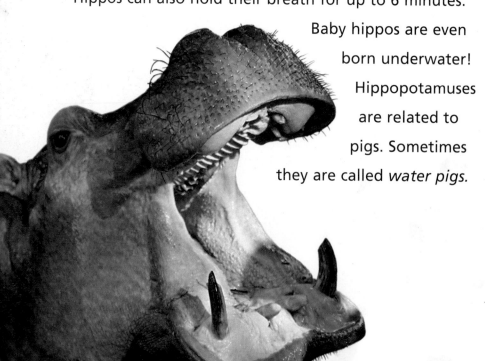

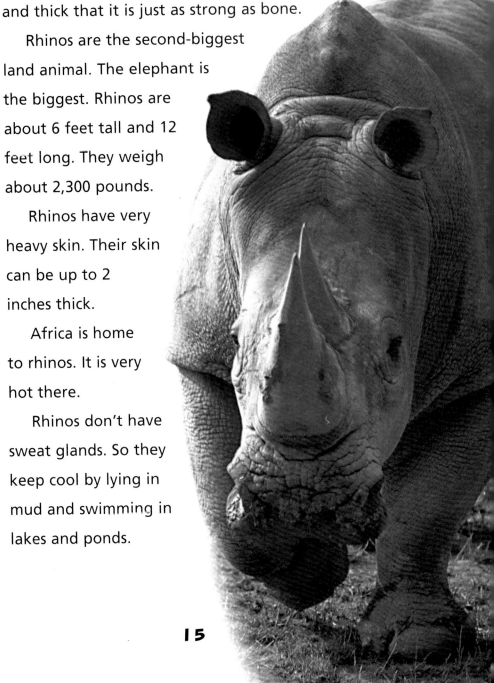

Rhinoceroses

Did you know that rhinos' horns aren't made of bone? They are made of hair! But this hair is so hard and thick that it is just as strong as bone.

Rhinos are the second-biggest land animal. The elephant is the biggest. Rhinos are about 6 feet tall and 12 feet long. They weigh about 2,300 pounds.

Rhinos have very heavy skin. Their skin can be up to 2 inches thick.

Africa is home to rhinos. It is very hot there.

Rhinos don't have sweat glands. So they keep cool by lying in mud and swimming in lakes and ponds.

15

Vulture

Chapter Two

Birds

Birds are the only animals that have feathers. Feathers help birds fly. But a few birds can't fly because they are too heavy.

Birds are warm-blooded animals. This helps them live all over the world. They are found in places that are both hot and cold.

Birds are *vertebrates.* That means they have backbones. Most bird bones are hollow. This makes birds lightweight so they can fly.

These animals do not give birth to live young. Instead, they lay eggs. Baby birds, or *chicks*, develop inside the egg.

Many different birds live on our planet. Let's meet some that are very unusual!

Ostriches

Not all birds fly. One bird that can't is the ostrich.

Ostriches are too big to get off the ground! These giant birds can be 9 feet tall. They weigh about 330 pounds. Their wings are just too small to carry all that weight!

Ostriches may not fly. But they sure can run! These birds have long, strong legs. Ostriches can run about 40 miles per hour.

During fights, ostriches use their powerful legs to kick enemies.

Ostriches live on the grasslands of Africa. They have no teeth. So they gulp down food in big mouthfuls. Ostriches also swallow small stones to break down the food in their stomachs. What a crazy way to eat!

Hummingbirds

There are many different types of hummingbirds. But they are all tiny! The smallest hummingbirds are only 2¼ inches long. They weigh less than a penny!

Hummingbirds hang in one place in the air while they sip *nectar*. That's a sweet liquid found inside flowers. Hanging in one place is something most other birds can't do.

Tiny hummingbirds also lay tiny eggs. Vervain hummingbirds lay the smallest eggs of any bird. Their eggs are less than ⅖ of an inch long. Their nests are about half the size of a walnut shell.

Pelicans

Pelicans have crazy-looking mouths! Special pouches hang under their beaks. Their pouches hold the fish they catch.

Pelicans "fish" by diving into the water with their mouths open. They scoop up big mouthfuls of water and fish. Then they point their beaks down to drain out the water. All that's left is a pouch full of tasty fish!

Pelicans swallow the fish whole. The one thing these birds' big mouths don't have is teeth.

Vultures

Vultures are *scavengers*. They don't kill their own prey. Instead, they eat dead or dying animals. Scavengers are important because they keep the world clean.

Vultures' bodies look weird. But they are perfectly suited for their scavenger lives.

These birds have no feathers on their heads. That's because their heads get covered with blood while they are eating. Any feathers on their heads would get pretty dirty!

Vultures also have long necks to reach inside dead animals. And their hooked beaks are strong enough to rip off pieces of flesh.

Flamingos

Here's a crazy way to eat—upside down! Flamingos hold their beaks upside down in the water. Then they suck in water and mud with their tongues.

But flamingos don't eat the mud. They eat tiny shrimp, algae, and plants that live in the mud.

These birds suck out all the good food. Then they spit out the water and mud.

Flamingos have very long legs. Their legs help them wade through the water.

There are 18 different kinds of penguins. All of them live in the southern half of the world.

Penguins can't fly. But they are great swimmers! They use their wings like flippers to move quickly through the water.

Emperor and king penguins are the largest types. They are about 4 feet tall.

Both of these birds live in the waters around Antarctica. They have lots of body fat to keep them warm in the freezing temperatures.

Emperor and king penguins have special ways to take care of their chicks. Females lay the eggs. Then the males place the eggs on top of their feet. They keep the eggs there for up to 2 months!

Meanwhile, the females head off to sea to eat fish, squid, and shrimp. By the time they return, the males are skinny and tired. Now it's the males' turn to go off and eat. So the females care for the eggs.

Penguins are great swimmers. But they aren't very good walkers. Their legs are just too short. Instead, emperor and king penguins slide across the ice and snow on their bellies!

Hornbills

Hornbills have big, heavy beaks. The first two bones in their necks are joined together to support their beaks!

Hornbills build crazy nests to protect their eggs. Females find holes in trees. Then they use mud to seal themselves and their eggs inside. Their mates pass food into the nests through small holes. Females and their chicks stay inside the nest until the chicks are old enough to fly.

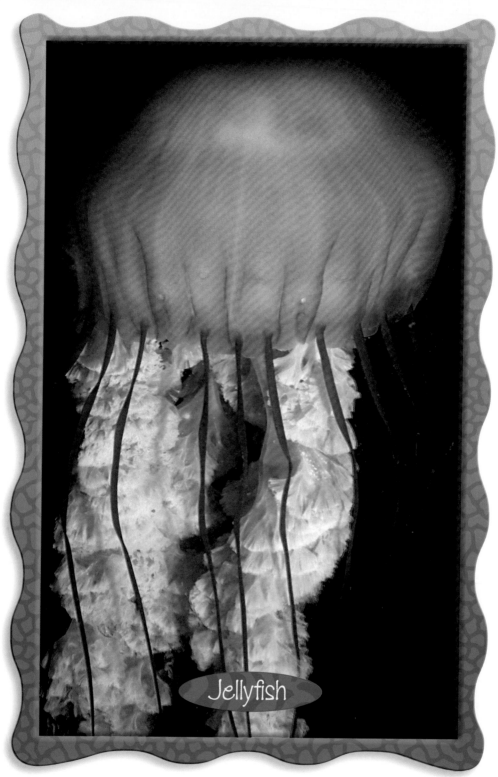

Jellyfish

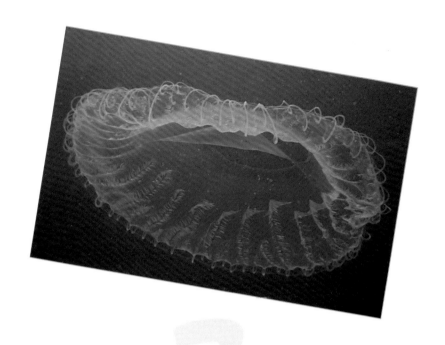

Chapter Three

Sea Creatures

Many different creatures live in the sea. Some are mammals. They have to surface to breathe. Others are fish. They breathe underwater through their gills. And still others are *invertebrates*. Invertebrates do not have backbones.

Living underwater means that sea creatures have special ways to survive. Some of these ways are pretty crazy!

Squids

Squids are the largest invertebrates in the world. Giant squids can be about 20 feet long and 6 feet wide. The largest one ever discovered weighed more than 2 tons.

Squids have strange-looking bodies. They have no bones at all! Instead, their bodies are protected by shells.

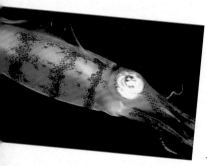

But those shells aren't on the outsides of squids' bodies. They're on the insides. Squids' bodies seem to be inside out!

Another odd thing about squids is their huge eyes. Some giant squids' eyes measure almost 16 inches across. That's larger than any other animals' eyes.

Squids don't swim the way other sea creatures do. They fill their bodies with water. Then they spray the water out from tubes under their heads. The force of the water pushes them along.

Squids can also squirt black ink into the water. This ink makes it hard for other animals to see them.

Piranhas

These fish live in the rivers of South America. They are less than 12 inches long.

Piranhas look harmless. But they are among the most dangerous fish in the world. Look in their mouths and you'll see why!

These fish have lots of very sharp teeth. They have very strong jaws too.

Piranhas swim in large groups. As soon as they smell blood, the group attacks! A group of piranhas can strip the flesh off a large animal in seconds.

Lungfish

Lungfish don't breathe water like other fish do. Instead, they breathe air through special lungs. These fish must rise to the surface of the water to breathe.

If you think fish that breathe air sound crazy, what about fish that can live out of water?

Lungfish live in Africa where long periods of time pass without rain. So the fish *estivate*, or become inactive, during these dry seasons.

These fish burrow into the mud and curl into tight balls. They cover their bodies with mucus. Mud sticks to the mucus and forms hard cases that protect the fish.

Only a small hole is left in each case. Lungfish breathe through these holes.

When the rain comes, the cases soften. Then lungfish swim away.

Anglerfish

Have you ever heard of fish that go fishing? That's just what anglerfish do. Anglerfish have special fins on top of their heads.

A small piece of flesh called the *esca* hangs from the fins. The escas look like worms as they move in the water. When other fish come close to take a bite, the anglerfish gobbles them up!

Anglerfish also eat animals such as squid and crabs. But those animals are much bigger than anglerfish. How do the anglerfish do it? They stretch their stomachs until they are big enough to hold the prey.

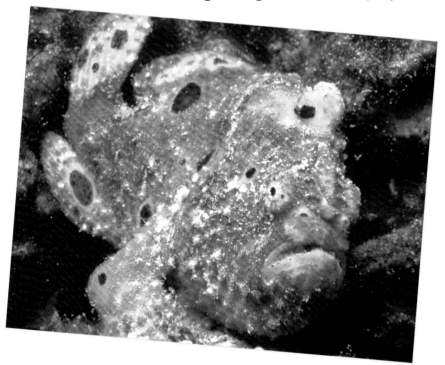

Puffer Fish

When puffer fish are threatened, they swallow huge amounts of water or air. Their bodies blow into big, round balls. This sudden change usually scares away predators.

Puffer fish have other ways of protecting themselves. Their bodies are covered with poisonous mucus that can kill other fish.

One type of puffer fish is called the porcupine fish. They are covered with sharp spines. These spines pop out when the fish puff up their bodies.

These animals look a lot like horses. But they are actually fish. Their odd-looking bodies help them in several ways. Sea horses suck tiny animals into their long, narrow mouths. And they use their tails to hold on to seaweed.

Probably the craziest thing about sea horses is that the males carry the eggs. Females lay their eggs in a special pouch on the males' body. Then the males carry the eggs until they hatch.

Jellyfish

These creatures don't really look like animals at all. Jellyfish have no bones in their bodies.

Jellyfish move by puffing their bodies open and closed. This squeezes water out from under their bodies. The force of the water pushes jellyfish along. If jellyfish stop

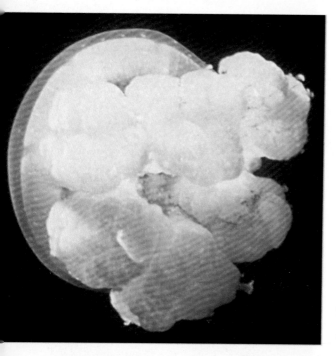

moving, they sink!

Their mouths are on the bottom of their bodies. They are surrounded by long tentacles covered with poisonous stingers.

These animals catch small fish, shrimp, and crabs in the tentacles around their mouths. They paralyze the prey with poison. Then they pop the food into their mouths.

Jellyfish stings can hurt people too. Some jellyfish found near Australia are very poisonous. Their poison can kill a person in less than 3 minutes!

Starfish

Starfish like to eat coral. But their mouths are too small to take in large pieces. So how do the starfish eat? They push their stomachs out of their mouths and eat with their stomachs!

Starfish have no heads, tails, fronts, or backs. Their bodies are circular. Arms grow out of a central disk. The central disks control their bodies. Another crazy thing about starfish is they can grow new body parts. If one arm is cut off, starfish will grow a new one. And if enough of the central disk is attached to the cut-off arm, a whole new starfish will grow!

Iguana

Chapter Four

Reptiles

Reptiles are *cold-blooded*. That means their bodies are the same temperature as the air around them. They can't control their body temperatures. So if cold-blooded animals get too hot or too cold, they will die.

These animals keep warm by staying in the sun. They cool off by moving into the shade, crawling under rocks, or swimming.

Reptiles don't give birth to live young. Instead, they lay eggs. These animals usually lay many eggs at a time. But they don't have to take care of their young. As soon as the babies hatch, they are able to find food and take care of themselves.

Reptiles first appeared about 250 million years ago. So these crazy creatures have been living on Earth for a long, long time.

Boa Constrictors

Constrict means to "squeeze" something. Boa constrictors squeeze their prey to death. But they don't crush their prey. Instead, they squeeze the prey's bodies so hard that the animals can't breathe.

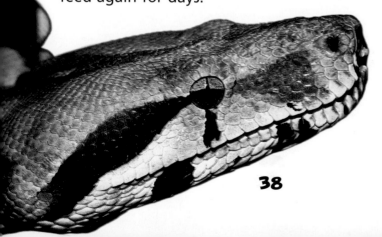

Snakes can't chew their prey. They must swallow their food whole! How do boa constrictors swallow large animals? These snakes can open their jaws very wide. Then strong muscles in their bodies move the prey into the snakes' stomachs. After snakes have eaten big meals, they do not need to feed again for days.

Komodo Dragons

Did you think dragons could only be found in fairy tales? Meet the Komodo dragons. These creature are real monsters!

Komodo dragons are the largest members of the lizard family. These big, heavy animals can grow to 11 feet long. And they can weigh up to 350 pounds.

Komodo dragons are fierce hunters. They have strong jaws and sharp teeth.

But one of the most dangerous things about the dragons is their saliva. It is full of bacteria and germs. If animals are bitten by Komodo dragons, they usually get very sick. Soon, they die. Then the dragons find the bodies and eat them.

Komodo dragons can kill prey much larger than themselves. They eat wild pigs and deer. Komodo dragons have even killed and eaten people!

Chameleons

Few animals are as strange as chameleons. These lizards have cone-shaped eyes that stick out from their heads. Each eye can move by itself. So chameleons can look at two things at the same time.

Chameleons' tongues are pretty crazy too. Their tongues can be as long as their bodies. They keep them curled up in the back of their mouths. But when insects fly by, chameleons' tongues shoot out with lightning speed. Their tongues smack the insects and drag them into the chameleons' mouths.

One of the craziest things about chameleons is that

they can change color. This happens when the light or temperature around them changes. They also change color when they are excited or scared.

Iguanas are pretty big. One type, the green iguana, can grow up to 6 feet long. But these large lizards don't move very fast. They're happy to sit still on warm logs all day long.

Iguanas are *herbivores*. That means they eat only plants. An iguana's favorite foods are fruit, leaves, and flowers.

Iguanas are usually brightly colored. Their bodies are covered with flaps of skin. Sharp spines cover their backs and tails. These flaps and spikes look crazy. But they protect the iguanas from predators.

Iguanas use their tails to protect themselves. They swing their tails like clubs to scare predators away.

Gila Monsters

These animals aren't really monsters. They just look like monsters!

Actually, Gila monsters are lizards. They live in the deserts of the southwestern United States and northern Mexico.

Gila monsters are poisonous. Poison flows into their mouths from glands in their lower jaws. When these lizards bite other animals, the poison comes out of grooves in their teeth and kills their prey.

Gila monsters store fat in their tails. So if they can't find anything to eat in their desert home, they can live off the fat in their tails.

Geckos

These little lizards can do some crazy things! Geckos have sticky pads on their toes. These pads help geckos stick to things. That means they can walk up walls and across ceilings!

Another crazy thing about these animals is that they have no eyelids. So geckos keep their eyes clean and wet by licking them with their long tongues!

More than 750 types of geckos live in the warm parts of the world. Many people also keep these lizards as pets.

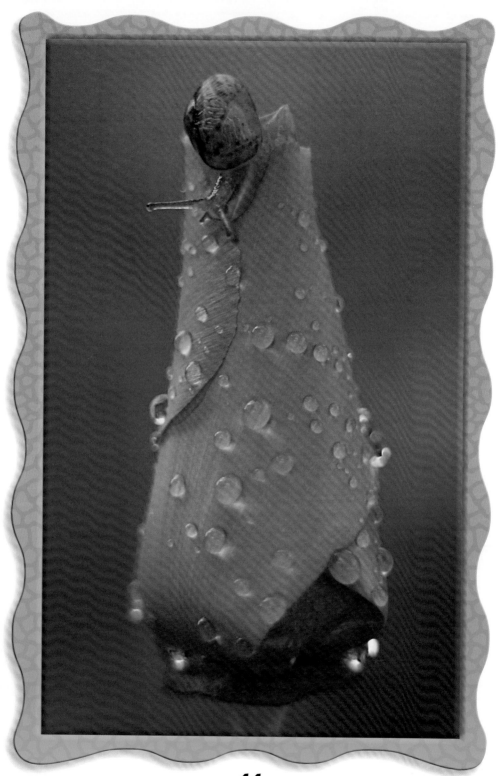

Chapter Five

Snails, Insects, and Spiders

Snails

Imagine having teeth on your tongue and a foot on your stomach. Then imagine leaving a trail of gooey slime wherever you go. Finally, think about moving only 160 feet per hour. All this adds up to one really crazy creature—the garden snail!

Snails crawl by expanding and contracting a muscular foot on the bottom of their bodies. A special body part leaves thick trails of slime. This slime helps the snails slide along.

Snails also have hard shells on their backs. These shells protect them from danger. Snails quickly pull their heads and feet inside the hard shells to escape predators.

Snails also crawl inside their shells to hibernate during the winter. They plug up the openings with slime and stay inside their moist home until spring.

Insects are small animals that breathe air. They are *arthropods*. Arthropods are invertebrates that have jointed legs, segmented bodies, and hard shells called *exoskeletons*.

Insects' bodies are divided into three parts—their heads; their *thoraxes*, or chests; and their *abdomens*, or stomachs. Most insects also have six legs, two antennae, and four wings.

Insects can live almost anywhere. They can even live in places that are very hot or very cold. In fact, there are more insects on Earth than any other type of animal. Scientists have found about 1 million species so far.

Stink Bugs

Stink bugs really do stink! These insects have large scent glands on the bottom of their bodies. When they are

in danger, they squirt a nasty-smelling liquid from these glands. The bad smell usually scares predators away.

Stink bugs also protect themselves by camouflage. Stink bugs that eat plants usually have green bodies. Because their bodies are the same color as the plants, it's hard for other animals to see them.

Dung Beetles

You probably wouldn't want to eat animal droppings, or *dung*, for dinner. But you would think those droppings were pretty tasty if you were a dung beetle.

Dung beetles also lay their eggs in animal waste. These insects roll the droppings into balls. Then they push the balls into burrows, or holes in the ground.

The beetles lay their eggs in the balls. When the eggs hatch, the baby beetles will have plenty of dung to eat.

Eating dung sounds disgusting. But it's actually very important. By eating animal waste, dung beetles help keep the world clean.

Have you ever heard cicadas singing on a hot summer night? These insects can be heard more than ¼ of a mile away. Male cicadas vibrate special parts of their bodies to make sounds. The males use these sounds to attract females during mating season.

Adult cicadas only live about six weeks. That's just long enough to mate and lay eggs. But the *larvae*, or babies, live underground for up to 1/ years! This strange life cycle is why some cicadas are called *17-year locusts*.

Praying Mantises

These insects hold their long front legs up in front of their bodies. But they aren't praying. They are waiting for dinner to come along! When other insects fly past, praying mantises snap their legs over their victims and push them into their mouths.

Praying mantises will attack any insects. They will even attack other praying mantises! When males want to mate with females, they must move slowly and carefully.

Mosquitoes

Mosquitoes are found almost everywhere on Earth. They fly around the warm, wet jungles near the equator. They are even found on top of the world in the frozen areas of the Arctic Circle!

Only female mosquitoes bite. Females have large mouths that can pierce skin and suck blood. Male mosquitoes have small mouths. Males only eat water and sweet flower nectar.

Did you ever wonder why mosquito bites itch so much? Female mosquitoes inject some of their saliva into bites. That makes blood flow quickly and easily. But the saliva also makes the skin swell and itch.

Mosquitos are very small. So females can't suck enough blood to kill a person.

But mosquito bites can spread terrible diseases. So many people have died of these diseases that mosquitoes are considered the deadliest animals in the world. Scientists think that mosquitoes have caused half of all human deaths in history!

Water Striders

These insects can walk on water! Water striders have long legs and light bodies. Their feet are covered with tiny, waterproof hairs. These hairs help them skate along the top of the water without getting wet. Water striders can even jump into the water without sinking.

Walking on water helps striders find food. When other insects fall into the water, striders grab them and gobble them up.

SPIDERS

Like insects, spiders are part of the arthropod family. But their bodies are different from insects. Spiders have eight legs. And their bodies are divided into two parts, not three. Finally, spiders have fangs, and most have poison glands.

Spiders and insects are common animals. But many of them are very unusual! Let's meet some of these crazy creatures.

Tarantulas

The tarantula is the largest member of the spider family. The largest tarantulas are called Goliath bird-eating spiders. They live in South America.

Bird-eating spiders are about 4 inches long. The distance between their legs can be up to 11 inches.

These spiders really do eat birds. They snatch sleeping birds out of their nests with their long, strong legs.

Like most spiders, tarantulas are poisonous. When they bite their prey, they inject venom. This poison can paralyze the prey. It can even kill it.

Despite the fact that they are poisonous, some people like these crazy creatures. They even keep tarantulas as pets!

Jumping Spiders

Jumping spiders don't spin webs to catch their prey. These spiders have very strong legs. They can leap up to 40 times their own length. This great leaping ability helps these spiders jump on their prey. Then they inject their poison.

Jumping spiders have very good eyesight. Like other spiders, they have eight eyes.